# Future Rounds the Curve

Poems
by
Patricia Barone

BLUE LIGHT PRESS ◆ 1ST WORLD PUBLISHING

SAN FRANCISCO ◆ FAIRFIELD ◆ DELHI

## Future Rounds the Curve

Copyright ©2023 by Patricia Barone

All rights reserved. Printed in the United States of America. No part of this book may be used or reproduced in any manner whatsoever without written permission except in the case of brief quotations embodied in critical articles and reviews. For information contact:

1st World Library
PO Box 2211
Fairfield, IA 52556
www.1stworldpublishing.com

Blue Light Press
www.bluelightpress.com
bluelightpress@aol.com

Book & Cover Design
Melanie Gendron
melaniegendron999@gmail.com

Interior Illustrations
*Fire*, p. viii; *Water*, p. 26; *Earth*, p. 48; *Air*, p. 74
Melanie Gendron

Cover Art
"A Face on the Train," a wood block print made using a reduction block process by Patricia Barone

Author Photo
Barbara Strandell

First Edition

Library of Congress Cataloging-in-Publication Data

ISBN: 978-1-4218-3549-5

# Praise for *Future Rounds the Curve*

In *Future Rounds the Curve*, Patricia Barone speaks to us in a clear voice, about the passage of time, and how that journey urges us to live with fullness of the heart in this present moment. In narrative, lyric meditations, she brings to life family, friends, animals, birds, childhood and later life experiences, bravely sharing her delight, pain, love, loss, and hard-earned epiphanies. "It's funny how time expands / when distance contracts..." These poems are about the life of the soul. "Your cravings of body and spirit: / Record them, your last testament. / Rise up and sing for small joys." Praising the natural world of flowers, bees, cicadas as a symphony, she offers us her simple wisdom: "Love your life." These beautifully written, powerful poems will endure. Patricia Barone needed to write this book, for herself, and those she loves. We need to read it, that we might glimpse reflections of our own lives, in hers.

   – Michael S. Moos, poet and author of *The Idea of the Garden*, winner of the Richard Snyder Publication Prize

In *Future Rounds the Curve*, Patricia Barone has united poems of the personal – family, love and loss – with poems that engage the larger world and its chaos. The poem *Why* questions war: "In Ukraine, where rockets/ plow the fields." The poet admits her limits. "Distressed by others' pain,/ I feel futile rage/ and turn away." After a Black man is murdered by a white policeman, "shadows spread like blood." In *Time's Spiral*, she describes the isolation of the Pandemic. "No breathing in/ someone else's breath./No more touching." Her poems describe borders – between the visual and the visionary, the ordinary and the ineffable. In *You Will Morph*, the only future is further change. "Next is not your death/ but your transformation:// The itch you've scratched/beneath each scapula/ will be wings,/ healing lesion,/ or grace unforeseen.// Urgent as your heartbeat." This is a book of fragile hope in a shared and threatened world.

   – Mary Kay Rummel, author of *Nocturnes: Between Flesh and Stone*

In her new book of poetry, *Future Rounds the Curve*, Patricia Barone imaginatively examines her past, her long marriage, children, travel, and always nature in its many forms – a monarch butterfly, a river turtle, "an ecstasy of bees." These are poems written from her experience, passion, and facility with language. Her intentions are to gently instruct the future – her children, nieces and nephews – each named in the dedication – "Don't shiver waiting for angels/ to stir the river or warm the ocean." In the end, her simple but profound invitation to the reader resonates with the conviction and example of her own approach to poetry and life – Love your life.

– Tim Nolan, author of *Lines*

In *Future Rounds the Curve*, Patricia Barone reminds us of "how wide and deep love is." The span of her life on this blue planet entwines with water, fire, soil, salt, air and community. These poems, like her black dog, "roll [their] fur in soil and nestle on her unmade bed." They invite us to see ourselves on this journey she has forged with her family. Like the mighty Mississippi, time flows like an arrow, all too fast from birth to death, but her poet's eye captures these moments again and again – of sorrow and joy – more like a circle. If we listen real close, we might hear the Banshee sing.

– Kevin Patrick Sullivan, author of *Unimpaired*

*With love, I dedicate this book
to my children, nieces and nephews*

Matt • Claire • Michelle • Kim • Melissa • Bill • Ruth • Lynn
• Kate • Lauren • Claire • Peter • Leonie • Emme

## Acknowledgements

"Times Arrow," *Adult Children*, a Wising Up Press anthology

"Unfolding my Death, I Said," *Poets On: Escaping*

"There Will Be No Holy Place," *Improbable Worlds: an anthology of Texas and Louisiana Poets*, Mutabilis Press

"You Will Morph," an award finalist. *New Millennium Writings, the 25th Anthology*

"Making Bone Lace," *Surprised by Joy*, a Wising Up Press anthology

"Your Destination Will Be the Story You Tell," *Crosswinds Poetry Journal*, Vol. 5

"Your Spirit Comes into Being Because of Your Body," *Crosswinds Poetry Journal*, Vol. 6

"Ten Days After His Murder," *Pandemic Puzzle Poems*, Blue Light Press

"Bees Invitation," *Pandemic Puzzle Poems*, Blue Light Press

"A Face on the Train," *Canyon, River, Stone and Light*, Blue Light Press

"A Dancer's Arc Will Sustain You," *Canyon, River, Stone and Light*

"Forever Returning in the Light," *Crosswinds Poetry Journal*, Vol. 8

"Old Wisdom Will Save Us," *Monterey Poetry Review*, Fall 2022

"Sight," *Monterey Poetry Review*, Fall 2022

"My Black Dog," published in a photograpy exhibit, *Vernacular Bestiary* by John Nicols

# Table of Contents

## Journeys of Instinct and Desire

To Those I Missed Along the Way .................... 1
Using Space, the Hollow Tube of Time ............... 3
Your Destination Will Be the Story You Tell ......... 4
Mariposa on Their Perilous Journey .................. 6
River Turtle ........................................ 7
Ferment Follows Desire .............................. 9
My Black Dog ....................................... 10
Let Nature Take Her Course ......................... 12
Your Muse .......................................... 13
A Dancer's Arc ..................................... 14
A Face on the Train ................................ 15
After Gram Dies, Enough ............................ 18
Does Every Excess Become a Vice? ................... 20
When Everyone Comes Your Way, Stay ................. 22
Blessed Are the Lazy ............................... 23
Let It Be .......................................... 24

## How Wide and Deep Love Is

Pacing Your Life for Love .......................... 27
Beginning of Our Story's End ....................... 29
Home Movie ......................................... 30
Small Neighborhood in the Cosmos ................... 32
Wind, Moon, and River .............................. 34
Adjoining Rooms .................................... 35
His Last Meal ...................................... 36
Life in Grief ...................................... 37
Painting You in Timelessness ....................... 38
Time's Arrow ....................................... 39
Transformation ..................................... 40
Their Scrying Glass ................................ 41
Quiet at the Center of the Wind .................... 43

She Puts on Her Low-Down Blues .................................. 46
Connection ......................................................................... 47

## When World Sorrow Brings Us Low

Drifting Back with Goldeneyes ......................................... 51
The Old Woman and the Sparrow ................................... 52
At a Wistful Distance ........................................................ 54
Time's Spiral ...................................................................... 55
Why ..................................................................................... 56
Be Extremely Subtle, Even to the Point of Formlessness .... 58
Shelling .............................................................................. 60
Motion and Rest ............................................................... 62
Rape .................................................................................... 64
The Age of Reason ............................................................ 65
Silence that Conceals Will at Last Expose ....................... 67
After His Murder .............................................................. 69
Final Loss Beneath the Sun .............................................. 70
When World Sorrow Brought Me Low .......................... 71
How You Go On ............................................................... 72

## Transformation: Luminous Body & Earth-Loving Soul

There Will Be no Holy Place Where You Are Absent ........ 77
Forever Returning ............................................................. 78
Making Bone Lace ............................................................ 80
Late Summer Woman ....................................................... 81
Time Exposure ................................................................... 83
Wonder ............................................................................... 85
All Senses Come Alive ...................................................... 87
Your Spirit Comes into Being Because of Your Body ...... 89
Through her Permeable Body .......................................... 90
Living in Flux, Being at Rest ............................................ 91
In My Midsummer Night's Riddle .................................. 92
You Will Morph ................................................................ 93
Invitation ........................................................................... 94

About the Author .............................................................. 97

Journeys of Instinct and Desire

# To Those I Missed Along the Way
*After Chuck Close's painting, 'Big Self Portrait'*

"Must be sick or dead." At eighty-six,
my mother, all her wits about her,
wasn't surprised when an older friend
forgot her birthday, stopped calling.

Behind my mom on a gradual –
then sudden – path to death,
I want to find my misplaced friends.

Maybe an almost-lover
who left for Brazil,
Tobago, or the Netherlands.
Tonight I'll call, invite him
to fill the screen of my mind.

If he visits, he'll be larger
than the youth I knew,
the many selves he hid.
His global empathy will move me.

Like the nine-foot high
Chuck Close self-portrait.
Far away, it appears to be
a *photo* of Chuck, but near
as you can get without a blur,
his features are rendered
in spheres or pixels.

He is a painted multitude –
each cell of himself
another person.

Close, closer,
the pores of his face
are shallow basins holding
all the people I never knew
or loved enough –
all waving their hands.

## Using Space, the Hollow Tube of Time

Bats send sonic waves
to search the world.
They echolocate prey
and echo-sound
caverns of the human mind for meaning.

When a cauldron of bats transmits,
I hear pings and typing –
tap, tap, tap but faster –
insistent summons from a cloud of seekers.

Heeding their appeal, I cease
stirring my nightly stew of worries.
I rally and send my spirit to converse
with people who pray though they don't believe.

Our songs and cries rebound
from ever steeper cliffs.
Our ululations return to us with news:
We live the doppelgänger's dream –
being here and there at once.

Lying in bed, listening to bats overhead,
I'm also in the kitchen where water drops
dance on a sizzling stove.

Where all the bowls, dates, tasks
and people I've dropped inadvertently
call back from the mound of echoing shards –

Here          Still here              Be still

                Listen

# Your Destination Will Be the Story You Tell

You told your stories to everyone
until your voice grew hoarse.
After scratching tales in sand,
you baked them in clay.

Waves and gravity altered them –
sluiced sand and shattered tablets.
Only two of the ways
the world erases words.

Earthquakes split the cliffs,
shearing off obsidian.
You chose coral-flecked flint,
a tool you used incising marble.
Carving stone went slow and hard.
Wood decayed to punky splinters.

You stomped papyrus reeds into a scroll,
but words fell bleached and brittle in the sun.
Tanners stretched hides into parchment
for ink, distilled from cuttlefish.
Though you plucked
your quill from a goose's tail,
even vellum sprouted mold and buckled.

From China, Ts'ai Lun sent paper he made
from mulberry's inner bark
and tender bamboo,
beaten to mash in water –
sheets so smooth they carried mortals,
gods and goddesses, into any random fire.

Now your AI-fables replicate in air.
Expect cyber-trolls, crashes, wizards
hacking your image, viruses implanting
malware, worms to consume your words.

You'll guard your site and multiply,
dispersing text across the living Web.
Will you be happy? Click the page.

## Mariposa on Their Perilous Journey

Monarchs waft their golden cloud
to hover over a bleak field.
Splendid quintuple milkweed flowers
shredded by the plow.

Butterflies rise and wheel away,
leaving one butterfly's trembling
wings fanning silky pollinia
on the only milkweed left.

As the migrating orange balloon
loses air above Sierra Madres,
butterflies descend to Michoacan
beneath a waning gibbous moon.

Oyamel firs weep their needles
for two Methuselah Monarchs,
who may mate if they settle here.
Or not – such misfortune!

Instinct, thwarted by a gale,
is not deterred by snowflakes,
each crystal refracting infinite
chaos, where luck resides.

# River Turtle

The blade strikes rock,
twanging like a tuning fork,
in black clay so dense
the shovel handle
judders against my palms.

I knead the clay
to form a heavy ball
then pull out a head so old
its ancestors lived millennia
before Noah sailed the Flood.
Turtle's hooded eyes
weigh my worth.

Hissing, she snaps
her sharp beak shut
and lets me sculpt
each horny scute of shell.

Down the Mississippi's canyon wall,
her claws clutch and release
each century she passes.

As she grunts and sighs
on the dry, pebbled bed, the river
gushes from beneath her carapace.

Extending her neck and beak
like a prow, she glides
the amber water down
a sink hole in cracked mud.

She plunges past the mismatched

rock-stripes of earthquakes,
molten squiggles
of dead volcanoes
to bottomless sea.
I'd dive there if I dared.

## Ferment Follows Desire

Borne on a wave, *andante*,
to a salt marsh full of reeds,
a tiny pregnant mermaid scans
the beach for a temporary home.
*Lento, lento*, a hermit crab leaves
its feather-oyster shell – her shelter.

Waiting in this iridescent cavern,
she hears the clicks and keenings
of porpoises leaping in the ocean.
The lovesick sperm whale bellows.
Groans of blue-baleen cetaceans
rumble over the ocean floor.

Fathoms below, singing season
rouses the humpback whale.
His fluid whistles pierce her
borrowed shell. It opens.

She wakes, but it's not
the humpback's knocks,
nor his imitation
of an opening door.

It *is* the rush and push
of rude, bawling life.

## My Black Dog

Kettle, her body whipping
back and forth upon her tail,
tramples, snaps the sweet peas.
Though she'll get a scolding
she runs to me. Avoiding
my eyes, she presents
her wagging haunch
to be scratched.
She steps lightly
over her morning's
warm, orange turds,
and rests her paws
in the tulip border.
Snout inside the red
African Queen, she licks
its sticky anthers. Lapping nectar
down the row, she lifts pollen
from each yellow Dutchman.

Cleaning under her tail,
furious at worms or fleas,
she bites at her hair, even air.
When I stumble, scrape my skin,
she drags her rough tongue
softly over my knee.

Summer, I close the door,
but she punctures the screen,
begging in. Winter, she etches
the glass with her nails, and light
seeps out in a steam-dull smear.
My shoes are wet and loose

upon my toes. She chews
my straps and drools
upon my inner soles.

Snuffling fresh-raked dirt,
she dives, kicking leaves higher.
Her shoulders follow her nose
beneath my peonies.

Out! I yell,
but I have let her in.
She rolls her fur in soil
and nestles on my unmade bed.

## Let Nature Take Her Course

The stranded penguin,
asleep on her floe of ice,
waits for the sluggish Yukon's
freeze: Strait latches onto bank,
and she waddles to shore.

*A bear plods up*
*your neighbor's shingles*
*till his claws dislodge*
*a clump of snow.*

Looking for her rookery,
the penguin passes your house,
turns back toward the weeping
creak of your weathervane.

*Skidding, the bear slides fast*
*on his matted haunches*
*to soffits, the edge*
*of his world.*
*He digs in to climb again.*

The penguin is amazed –
your wind-sock puffs
with a blizzard-bearing
blow from home,
the sound an echo
of her mate's song,
his whole body calling her.

*You may keep the bear*
*from crashing through*
*your sod-roofed bungalow.*

Do not interrupt
the penguin's journey.

## Your Muse

An infant, you began
mapping your desires
on your hands, feet, and lips.
Her milk released you in your pleasure –
an artist because of your hunger.

Only in the space between
her visits to your dreams,
do you want to bring her,
white-headed, unassuming,
to your home. She'll eat
the porridge you provide,
page through your scrapbooks,
the blueprints you keep revising.

Each night you pencil in loops
or add another interchange.
You go farther, past the place
she wants you to let her off –
a weathered cabin.

She begs, "Please turn around.
I need to rest."

You tell her, "Not quite yet.
we're almost there."

# A Dancer's Arc

1.
Staking perfect insteps on a high jeté,
she soars above applause,
alights on the lake of Lir
where his children swim,
swans on a polished mirror.

Floating her leg behind her, she extends
her pliant arm and clever hand
to pluck the black swan's feather –
arabesque by a lake of tears.

Coloratura of the dance,
she sings ever higher meeting silence
above the highest G, the silence
allowing her to fold her wings
around her face to die.

2.
How will she pay tomorrow?
With shin splints,
the longer lines of injury
she'll dance through?

She'll hire herself again
for Phoenix play.
Torn obliques won't heal
in the fire her toe shoes spark.
She'll scatter plumes of ashes when she leaps.

# A Face on the Train

*As I worked, I remembered her strong face*

Before the train pulled out of Ljubljana,
a mother and daughter, in babushkas
and mud-flecked raincoats, scrambled on
without luggage, short of breath.
On a cracked leather seat, they faced me.

*To begin a reduction print, I must*
*know where the light will rest.*
*I cut my wooden block*
*to keep the white of her forehead,*
*the moonlit stroke of her nose,*
*plateau of her chin,*
*the way the pebble path*
*winds through her hair.*

A man retrieved his suitcase to leave,
murmuring Slovenian-inflected English,
"The young one – she's famous on TV."

The celebrity, her face pale, leaned forward.
"Please hide this purse full of dinars.
Too much for vacation, the guard will know!
We're forbidden to remove them under Tito."

*I push my roller through gold.*
*It covers the fields with buckwheat,*
*burnishes stained glass windows,*
*and follows the curve of the street –*
*tiled roofs, shut doors,*
*their former home up hill.*

Just as I closed my knapsack,
the conductor, with a guard,
slid the door back too fast,
a snap of metal, as if to catch us.
I looked at the Tatras, Each peak
framed by our moving window.
He asked for my passport –
I fumbled in my handbag,
fingers brushing contraband.

*I excise the gold but leave ridges*
*to give the blue a green undertone.*
*On my transparent rice paper,*
*tears run down her cheeks.*

The guard turned to the women.
Babushka, mother, feigning sleep.
Her daughter laughed, as if at ease,
and signed her autograph. I caught
"Koper," a Yugoslav coastal city.

*I whittle cerulean blue from wood*
*to keep it on the paper. Pulling*
*the prints, I try not to smear*
*the sky, reflected on her cheeks.*
*I'm happy the way amber*
*puts a shimmer on white.*

After the guard and conductor
left, with slanting glances back,
the daughter, her gaze steady,
bowed as I returned her purse.

*I carve what is left of the block.*
*Lines trace the road they took.*

*She almost carried her mother.*
*Sable ink delineates their loss.*
*Linden trees, the hidden*
*steeple of the church.*

*Spiked metal doesn't conceal*
*the Adriatic sea as it laps*
*the coast of Italy.*

The two escaped by boat
when the moon's dark curve
concealed a daughter rowing
her mother to Trieste.

# After Gram Dies, Enough

*For Claire*
*In Irish 'enough' is 'go leor.'*
*In English, it became galore.*

Aunt Hilaire, in the seven-channel chair,
called us young ones over. I was twenty
and declined the painted figurines.
My mother, Blue, agreed, "too frou-frou."
Hilaire withdrew an oval stone,
dawn blue, from a satin-ribbed box.

Imbued with pink, this egg was dropped
by a prehistoric bird in a silver cleft.
When their steam train stopped
in Leadville, Colorado, Thomas,
your Great Grandpa, knelt down
and gently removed this petrified egg,
giving it to Great Gramma Lizzie.

My oldest cousin, Ellen, bent her head,
so Hilaire could fasten real pearls
at the nape of her neck,
Gramma's "only good jewelry."
I preferred the hard-won egg.

I was meaning to give my fossil,
one hundred and forty-years old
since found, to my daughter,
forty-four. But it's gone.
It hatched or rolled away.

Before I die, I'll sit soft
in the seven-channel chair
and ask my matriarchal dead –

Lizzie, Blue, Hilaire, and Ellen –
to help me select Claire's keepsake.

If I offer her my string of amber beads,
those thousand-year-old drops of resin
will release soothing oils to her skin.

If she wears the beads, she'll have enough
love to hand them on and luck galore
to welcome the blue egg home.

# Does Every Excess Become a Vice?

1. *Or Advice?*

Who can resist cracking open
a pink saccharine pastry to read
fortune disguised as advice –
a vise grip squeezing
your equanimity.
We give advice too easily.
When you savor a chocolate truffle,
foil wrappers don't chide you.


2. *Or a Virgin?*

The scent is gardenias
or Asian lilies.
Kiss the downy curve
before your teeth bite through
the taut rosy skin of your peach.
Before receiving the sacrament again,
cleanse your mouth with praise.


3. *Or a Revision?*

You layer a lasagna –
ricotta, mozzarella, pasta,
eggplant and caramelized onions,
tomato paste not sauce –
and eat it all alone.

Sorry for your lonely gluttony,
you tramp down a gravel road
to a chapel, a skull on the altar.
If you begin to brood, get out
your pencil. The pulpit
is your writing desk.

Your cravings of body and spirit:
Record them, your last testament.
Rise up and sing for small joys.
Water earth with large sorrows.
Forgive your bumbling self
and the juggler falling
off a pyramid of shoulders.
Be a tragicomic hero.

## When Everyone Comes Your Way, Stay

Your lap has never been full.
Your food is a still life –
one carrot, a slice of julienned leek,
two peas.

Why so self-effacing?
Were you forced to eat fried cactus?
Did you feel invisible,
the one in the middle,
*What's-his-name?*

Unfastening your beagle's muzzle
makes you glad, so you free
the skinny hamster from her treadmill.

Your pets invite guests:
Swarms of mason bees
wearing funny hats,
buzzing your tin shed,
enticing common toads.
Dandelions summon
a coven of hens.
Wearing camouflage, your dad.
Your mom in a 1950 house dress.

It's better if you don't leave
before the night's susurrations,
sighs of windy creatures,
luminous eyes on you,
the one they love.

# Blessed Are the Lazy

*after Claude Monet's waterlily paintings*

On Monet's oval pool, the wind
wrinkles a drift of white petals.
The naked in spirit wear
crimson waterlilies.

Archipelagos of lily-islands
cast shadows on water.
Shadows fly beneath clouds.
Cloud flying amuses the lazy.

The lazy will inherit time,
an invention of the busy.
Lazy folks, who prize
empty drawers, go naked.

Like mist ponds full of dew,
Monet's river runs shallow.
Lotuses dangle their roots,
gliding sedately downstream.

Indolent people, refusing to row,
float on rafts to the painter's bridge.
Ashore, they admire the lilies of the field,
which neither toil nor spin.

# Let It Be

If it's Elijah at the door, even God,
you wouldn't have to scrub the stoop
and vacuum cat hair. Just offer
your softest sofa and a glass of beer.

Angels join you on the ceiling
to gild the spiders' webs.
Boxelder bugs discretely die.
You see your inertia blessed.

The arthritis you use to excuse
your apathy? Your pain will be
preserved, each throbbing nerve
wound tight until you swallow
your mother's herbal remedy.

You'll do nothing more
to save yourself or the world
disappearing under snow.

Except for the fire you light,
your chimney's smoke
to guide your story home.

How Wide and Deep Love Is

# Pacing Your Life for Love
*in memory of Stan*

Traveling by Greyhound,
I'm passing burnished trees,
grass so alive my eyes slow
traversing each strand of green,
its sheen of crimson contradiction.

It's funny how time expands
when distance contracts – home to you.

~

Starting our conversation in the rain,
you hold the umbrella, dripping
New Orleans air on me.
We continue on the plane
to Zurich, its red roofs waiting.
I grab your hand as our plates ascend
and fall in another country.

~

The consequence of loving comes
when I'm panting to the beat
of my contractions.

You remind me to breathe.
My reply is earthy,
not like movie patter,
not Bacall to Bogart.

Slow as time-lapse,
you cut the baby's cord
and see blue shadows
around his nostrils.

The nurses take him away. I stay
awake, breasts swollen with milk.
Morning, he pinks in my arms.

After our daughter is born,
you hold her in water,
warm as my body.
She gazes into your eyes,
disclosing one of her mysteries.

~

Our small children watch the turtle
cross the yard a quarter way
to the fence by noon.

In their sleep they measure
reptilian progress 'til morning,
when they leave for work and college
before the turtle reaches the gate.

~

My husband, you make
the map of our lives
with your mindful hands,
securing our late-middle age,
which comes, springing up in the sun,
like clover in the turtle's wake.

# Beginning of Our Story's End

After he tells me, a cooling zephyr
lifts fine hairs on my arms.
My husband's feral white cells
multiply into our future.

Above us, a skein of starlings
unravels and rewinds –
fragile calligraphy.

With each implosion of feathers
inside the shivering ball they make,
their murmuration fills the air
with many voices.

Cold, I wrap my arms
on my breast and shut my eyes.
I hear a roaring waterfall.
Their wings are the water
and the rocks it crashes over.

My arms around his waist,
I whisper, *Listen.*
Rough flutters very near us –
black stragglers rise from the spruce tree
to join the roiling mass.

Wings tipping,
now black, now white,
they turn.

# Home Movie
   *for Matthew*

You are fourteen – your future
isn't waiting but unrolls
into the zillion milli-blips of light
your whirring camera captures.

As you kneel above us in the sleeping loft,
your video expands our dinner
the way a dancer pirouettes.

In Einstein's time, the quicker
the dancer turns, the slower time
in the center. From soup to coffee,
we grow younger sipping wine,
toasting Gram and Grampa,
married fifty years.

You shoot us in real time,
not a belch or cough left out.
With each click of glass on glass,
each tick of the railroad clock,
the dinner is blissfully boring.

Grandma's same old stories –
how she and her brother stole
a streetcar; how she never
won a medal skating
in the `32 Olympics.

All this, in the time it takes us to eat
sauerbraten, cheesy baked spuds,
green beans with almonds,
schaumtorte and coffee.

How you reel your elders in!
Your father's tonsure gleaming
in the candlelight, your mother
smoking – I can't deny it now.

It is, like always, a babble.
A voice briefly rising alone –
"She ate half the skin off our turkey" –
is swallowed in the hubbub of family.
Time flows through our throats,
an organ's pipes. The pressure of breath
releases our voices – tubas, groans,
oboes, piccolos and laughter.

After they uncork the Irish Cream,
your grandpa toasts your grandma.
Then she begins to clear away the torte.
Close up: her hands with their ropey veins.
"I'm not finished," Grandpa says, lighting
his one permissible Havana cigar.

The film runs out before smoke rises
to where your camcorder purrs.
So we'll never know exactly
when that dinner ended, if it did.

# Small Neighborhood in the Cosmos

*for Sharon, Mitchell's mother*

Sunrise, in his kayak, Mitchell
casts for Pacific jack mackerel.
Riding the waves off Pinõs Point,
he hooks a thrashing sea bass.

Succulents bow down, bob up.
Claire, my daughter, waters
cactus and euphorbia.
Her chihuahua dances,
his tongue hanging out
for the spray. He barks,
chipping at a flawless day.

Love apples crimson
as they climb an azure sky.
From raised beds, Claire selects
curly lettuce. She serves the fish
with creamy lemon sauce.

From over the fence, a neighbor
offers a platter of *carne guisada*,
declined, *muchas gracias*. Insisting,
he slides us generous portions.
We have room and heart for more –
food, family, and community.

Sharon and I lean back,
praising the feast, the leafy place
our children make together.

A black sky breaches for the sap moon,
light falling on coastal mountains,
beaches and this patio.

Cirrus streamers pass over.
Fleeting wraiths
on the landscapes of our faces.

Our homeplace, Planet Earth,
is tiny in deep space.

# Wind, Moon, and River

*For our children during the Corona virus*

Families aren't static in the album.
Slipping corner mounts, our photos curl.

Clouds scud across our skies,
as if a weary thumb moves years,
our changing images across a screen.

Under the spring's blood moon,
squalls weave between us.
We shiver beneath flailing trees.

May no harm come to you,
the two I once protected with my body.

The river is profoundly slow.
It keeps our lives, each a single day.
Years flow quick between our fingers.

## Adjoining Rooms

Storm cells gather up the heat,
releasing rumbles.

He opens her door,
puts his head against hers
and kisses her ear – she shivers.

Back in his room, he listens
to low reverberations, then
thunder/lightning together –
A bolt cleaves the poplar
by his open window.

She runs to his room.
– "Are you still alive?"
– "Still here for now."

Later, when he dies,
she inhales his final breath.

## His Last Meal

*for Claire*

After pushing away his bland, blanched foods –
whipped egg whites, pink Ensure, wobbly jello –
he sat up, face glowing, when you walked in
with pizza – salami, pepperoni, bacon, mortadelle.
Relishing three small slices, he ate them point first,
enjoying the crunch of brown crispy crust, blasé
about digesting it. After the two of you joked,
you said, *Aw Dad, It's good to see you eat.*
I loved you both too much to speak.

# Life in Grief

*in memory of Stan*
*for Kay and Mike*

Leaf shadows on the blinds
moved me to phone dear friends
a continent away, but they
were an hour from our door.

Hearing their car, I helped you sit up in bed.
Only one foot in life, you took a wheelchair
to the living room and said goodbye forever.

Now when I'm alone with your spirit,
I rest by the hearth, reflected in our windows.
Flames leap toward our past. I try to stay.
Still, as I close my book, I hear
cellos seep from the last pages –
a tone poem for me from you.

Despite your reassurance,
tears roll into my mouth,
onto my sore tongue. I taste
salt in my blood – that's life
after your death, but never mind.

We old survivors go on living
in echoing depots, where trains
are either too late or too early.
Comrades, we keep each other company
until we each depart on time.

Keeping our friends close
and you, your mortal wound,
I knew, I know – how wide and deep love is.

## Painting You in Timelessness
*to my late husband*

At the ivory horizon, mist devours
the lake's sapphire water; purple
loosestrifes circle a teal pond.
I stipple my home, once ours,
with lilac-gold, brush filled
with all the colors of hurt.

On the last humid day of fall,
this leaf-taking time, cumuli swell
with rain, washing your lawn chair.
Lightening tears open the empty air.
Sails unfurl in tints of phthalo blue.
I'm painting hours too light to bear.

In deepest shade, the sun burns through
my heart, beating out of time with yours.

# Time's Arrow
### *for Matt*

Monarchs flit among milkweeds.
Black and yellow caterpillars curl
beneath leaves, becoming jade green
chrysalides. We wait for one to thin
and break its lemon-banded crown.

"Butterflies live time's arrow,"
says my son, "eggs to pupae to chrysalis.
They fly in one direction at a time –
mostly to the future."

Pointing to my white hair, I laugh.
"If they fly too fast to the future,
they turn and flutter back to the past."

A lengthy and erratic trip by wing –
I'd rather catch time's rocket
to Stan, Matt's dad, alive and joking.

Sitting on Matt's pergola,
enclosed by purple morning glories,
we watch his dog prowling
the edge of the yard,
worrying trees for squirrels.

Maybe a butterfly's cycle
is more a circle than an arrow.
Metamorphosis happens
in marvelous ways.

"I've been talking," I say, "to your father.
He returned on time's arrow to tell you
he likes the way you built this deck."
"I've taken Dad inside me," Matt says.

# Transformation

*for our son at fifteen*

When you were neither young
nor old enough to keep
yourself steady,
you said no.
Not risking drugs,
you lost false friends.
Alone, you were bound
by your own black thoughts.
Afraid to break, you didn't trust
a kaleidoscope transformation –
your stronger self created
out of broken pieces.

You held your head in your hands,
so great the pain of being still inside
the loss that cracked you open,
so your future could rush in.

# Their Scrying Glass

1. *Apartment 51 E*
Her very bad dream is jumping
away from her future,
falling to her past –
all laid out for burial.

The monitor stares,
a blank yet hostile eye.
She's too young to see her face
breaking in a shattered screen
or pane of glass. Fearing

she won't fear the edge,
the slamming ground's crude mercy,
she shuts the window tight.
She doesn't want to die alone.

Outside, a warbler offers
a descending slide of melody.
At the window, her hands
knotted behind her back,
she stretches her neck to see.

2. *Apartment 53 E*
A young man picks *Exit*,
but meant to click *Enter*
to opt the alternate life
his avatar leaps so easily.
He can't own the game –
even his droids darkside him.

He feels the weight on his chest,
constricting breath.

His heart squeezes out
each drop of blood.
He thinks he doesn't want to be.

Outside, the warbler chips away
at focus inside his home office.
Coworkers – last year's photo on his desk –
aren't here, there, anywhere. Together, anyway.
Everyone used to meet at the Loon Café.

3. *Barriers, Almost Broken*

The warbler cannot chirp
after it flew, beak first,
to the other warbler caught
behind the man's unyielding air.

Losing yellow feathers,
it darts the woman's closed sky,
dashing its beak once more,
falling with its mate.

The warbler musters
a short flight, thumping down
on the young man's balcony. Will he
slide his door open and go out?

Does she have the courage
to push her window up,
extend her head
just far enough to speak?

# Quiet at the Center of the Wind

1. *First Night*
When the house swayed,
I was alone in a dormer room.
Dusty kitten statuettes
clicked together, skittered apart.

My fiancée snored below,
on a hide-a-bed sofa
unfolded in his mother's den.
We'd fled low ground, high winds
Uptown where we lived in sin –
We loved below the level of the sea.

Fierce winds forked the oak
from its roots. I curved around
my chest, bent legs, holding on
to myself, unable to rise
or hope I wouldn't die.

Nothing dramatic
would kill me. Being flat
on the bed, unable to choose
which pants to wear, or if
I'd dress at all. Go down
to eat, or flop on the couch,
hide my face in a cushion,
feeling too sad to cry.
With all desire and power gone,
a person might as well be dead.

A gull shrieked when a mighty gust
threw it at the cracking pane.

2. *Second Day*

As snakes swarmed from bayous,
I imagined the hiss of water
rising past the windows
of our New Orleans flat.
Here in Metairie, I dealt
Kings, Queens and Jacks,
the Hermit and Hanging Woman.
Stuck, I shuffled fast while his mother
chattered on. "How cozy inside!"
Then her willow crashed.

3. *Second Night*

We climbed the stairs to share my bed.
Almost unafraid of the hurricane,
I liked the way it turned me
inside out, prepared
for the eye's calm circle
where all sound ceased.
Weaker but lethal, the gales
revived, hauling the cyclone's
encore, a wall of storm and thunder.
Camille's tail whipped –
hailstones tattooing garden sheds.

We settled our heads on one pillow,
listening to a shower so soft I cried
then slept without waking in his arms.

4. *Third Day*

A bracing, high-pressure wind
swept through the broken window,
over our faces, and shocked me awake.
Inhaling a lungful, feeling light, I kissed him.

Relieved my pain had lifted, I wanted to be
where the sky, hard blue, didn't have a cloud.
Stretching my arms and back, I got to my feet,
and we went home, our house still whole.

Now sluggish, the wind nudged jaundiced leaves
on the rising flood, the Mississippi jostling trees
and bodies of people, whose lives
we didn't yet grieve.

## She Puts on Her Low-Down Blues

After she loses a child,
she dresses in her own death.
In time, she tugs off her denim shroud.
Spread on the lawn, it fades and seems to fray.

At least, it doesn't grow,
like her little girls' feet. Last year's sandals
shrink on a Goodwill shelf.
Her boys' sharp knees and elbows, always poking through
their clothes. Thrifty, she finds more at Savers.
She feels a tenuous cheer.

She sews night curtains, gathers the muslin on rods,
to push back the dark outside and in – what will her kids do
if she dies? She decides *no way* and endures the pain inside.
Nightmares in her shape and size won't trouble them –
She'll make sure.

Though life isn't easy to put on,
it stays as a rhythm –
lacing shoes, making do.
Life is loosey-goosey.
Loose as her children's corduroys.
She strokes the fabric's ribs. The channels in between
*must* be going somewhere.

She grows sashes beneath her floating ribs
to tie herself to every day, even though each passes.
Her ribs safeguard her heart; she'll protect her kids,
even after they are grown. Until she can't go on.
Then she *will* lie down in cotton,
unafraid of death or even love.

## Connection

I do not see you falling
and can't hold you, only hear
the timbre of despair
thinning your voice to nothing.
Everything – your breath.

Before you say goodbye,
please let me stay with you.
I croon my words in your ear,
not knowing what they are,
a flowing murmur of care
the sound of a river
or rustling wheat
surrounding a still field
within the warming wind.

# When World Sorrow Brings Us Low

# Drifting Back with Goldeneyes

*in early spring*

The animated ice floes on the river
are ducks with yellow irises,
black-capped heads,
and pony-tail wisps of feather.

They're called *Bucephala*,
like Alexander the Great's horse,
*Bucephalus*. "What's that mean in Latin?"
Beth Daley asked the Classics teacher.
Our dirty joke was the phallus part.
While we snickered, he looked pleased –
"It means a bull's head in Greek."
We all shrieked.

This evening I see flashes –
light glancing off the water
or perhaps the lenses
implanted in my eyes.

I am old. My thoughts drift
backward every sunset.

Goldeneyes dip and bobble,
between the floats
of packed snow,

cutting ruddy ice flakes
from the waves.

# The Old Woman and the Sparrow
*In the time of Covid 19*

1.

Two antique plum trees,
wild with sour, wizened fruit,
twist their branches over my yard,
where sparrows practice triplet notes.

2.

Before the hygienist cleans my teeth,
I ask if her children learn at home.
She replies, "my kids are in school."
"How do you feel," I persist,
"about their risk?"

"I don't know *how* to feel!"
She folds her arms. "How do *you* feel?"

I'm ashamed I'd asked.
"I don't have any grandchildren,"
I admit, "but I'd be afraid."

Like any nosy crone in a fairy tale,
I'm not quite a witch, just a woman
with neither chick nor child
in the boiling pot of soup.

3.

When I get home, I gasp to see
a Cooper's hawk on my railing.
The nearest plum tree quakes with peeps.

The hawk snaps its wide tail shut,
showing a striped flight pattern,
then plunges the foliage.

When the hawk bursts out,
I don't know if I see
a sparrow in its scalpel beak.

# At a Wistful Distance
*During Covid 19*

After a solitary winter,
we squint at faces,
too far to really see.
Why do I near you,
only to veer away?

The person we each see
is smaller, face pared
to cheekbones.

Sun reduces us,
wraps around our hips,
removing the mammal weight
of long, dim days.

"Please eat more,"
I say, "before you break
like a glass thermometer
in this cold spring."

Our voices reach
each other's ears.
"Take care
of yourself!"
"Be safe!"

# Time's Spiral
*In the time of Covid 19*

A child, you dance alone,
kicking up sand.

Then, in a hopscotch jump,
you land on five and six.

You find yourself teetering
on seventy not seven.

Throwing your beanbag on eighty,
you drop your pension.

Will you try to pick it up and fall,
smearing your chalk line?

~

Time spirals off kilter.
The smallest toxic entity
has changed the rules:

No breathing in
someone else's breath.
No more touching.

In Ring Around the Rosy,
our cheeks are full of posies.

Ashes, Ashes –
We all fall down.

# Why

*At the end of the story
do we die?*

Night is feathered
with mockingbirds.
I wake to the jeers
of blue jays.

*I'm so tired
of the moon.*
    ~

Swans curve down
like question marks.

A small child asks,
"who bent their necks?"

*Beneath a harmless sky,
I cannot say.*
    ~

In Ukraine, where rockets
plow the fields,
soldier-fathers, mothers,
and grandparents die. And children.
Alive but alone, they cannot cry.

*I wonder who
would break their necks?*

*Distressed by others' pain,
I feel futile rage
and turn away.*
    ~

Night quickens
the tubers and corms,
the fleshy roots
of our dormant lives.

Queries sprout
in burning earth.
Lost, I hear a voice –

*In the beginning was woman,*

*who grew God,*

*a child who wondered, Why?*

# Be Extremely Subtle, Even to the Point of Formlessness
### *after the 6<sup>th</sup> century C.E. author of The Art of War*

When speaking of war, Sun Tzu never cried.
*"Be crafty, self-effacing,"* he advised
as soldiers crawled beneath the fire
to trenches where they died.
∼
Warrior's bones
will be consumed
to ashes, floating
above the salted farms,
falling to seedless ground
on rainy afternoons.

Invading our airways, their dust becomes
a scrim between their slaughter
and our unknowing grief.
∼
The potter sculpting their monument
will loosen their limbs from death.
She throws a chunk of clay –
not kaolin and feldspar
but made of the generals
and their gods of plunder –
to the spinning table.

Her hands pull up a cone of it,
then pumping her leg,
kicking the pedal,

she centers her hands, plunges down
and eases the sides up firmly
between her palms,

shaping a man or woman
who won't dissolve
to please Sun Tzu.

# Shelling

*In memory of Lieutenant Colonel Eddie A. Bachhuber*

Between a corn and a barley field,
we saw a captive giant clam
displayed in a Quonset hut.
Dad had seen larger mollusks
in the Philippines, World War II.
"Are you a hero?" He spat, mumbled,
and never spoke of his war again.

I almost see the way my surgeon father
earned his Purple Heart before the last
battle, when random shelling took out
soldiers on Los Negros Island's beach.
Medics bearing wounded were strafed.
Nurses grabbed stretchers and ran,
stumbled back avoiding flack,
descended deep into a shell-hole
hospital – Surgery was covered by tarps
pulled taut over trunks of coconut trees.

My father incised a soldier's shoulder,
removing bullets. Before closing the wound,
he bathed it in sulfa antibiotic, hoping the kid
survived – His surgical team, imperfectly good
like him, was gutsy, tight as the sterile thread –
boiled in a grunt's canteen – for stitching
injuries: Corpsmen gave their blood
and tore up parachutes for sheets.

Still, shell-shocked troops came home
missing legs and arms. Or minds –
some treated their pain with heroin,
whiskey, wine and valium. Any drug
or anyone to numb them.

Too many died – a depth charge
charring the souls of those who lived,
grew old, unable to tell their children
what they'd seen and done in war.

# Motion and Rest

*after the gnostic Gospel of St. Thomas
and Homer's epic poem, the Odyssey*

Spinning thread from wool, Penelope,
you weave a pallid shroud, your duty
to your absent husband's father.
Each night, you unravel
what you wove.

Passing twenty years this way,
*you* lift the heddle, pull the shuttle.
*Odysseus* dallies with a goddess.

Your suitors whirl past,
but you refuse to catch a single ring –
they're only brass.

Your life could be heroic,
but what do you choose?

*Rest over Motion.*

~

Suppose, Penelope,
you only have one chance.
Cease your silly waiting for Odysseus.
Your daughter will be conceived
without his seed.

When he gallops home
with his henchmen,
they'll shave her head
then drape her face and body
in yards of opaque veil.

So what will you choose?

*Motion over Rest*

when they come to bind her feet
and mutilate her sex.

# Rape

*after Degas' painting, Intérieur*

He bars the door with the weight of his body,
heft of his boredom – her scruples waste his time.

She twists away, falls on a chair,
a *prie-dieu* any whore might use,
he thinks, though she is not. Just worn,
torn like her dress, cape and chemise.

He ignores her flesh. It's not desire
when he draws out his belt, undoes his fly.

# The Age of Reason

*After Van Gogh's "Church in Auvers"
and in grateful memory of Father Terrence*

Her stomach clenching like a fist,
she crosses sunlit clay
into a patch of darkness
where the church squats.

She wants to confess outside,
near trees, where the young priest
says her soul is white.

Not the old priest inside his box.
He asks what she does in bed,
in the bath, all her clothes off.

Seven years old, she is
the age of reason and can sin
the old priest says. Sins slip in,
even on her thoughts.

Sins pile up – she must go back,
must tell the old one who crouches
inside his fake black dress.

Each Saturday she leaves behind
the weight on her chest,
to sleep at home, not in hell.

A red light leaps – old spider waits.
She runs out of church and slams
the heavy door behind her.

The young priest's voice is kind –
"You worry – that's no sin."
She trusts in his red hair, blue eyes.

The old priest's eyes sink in
so deep, she can't see any light.
She runs back and drags
his curtains down –
"No! goodbye forever!"

# Silence that Conceals Will at Last Expose
*Upon the defeat of Roe v. Wade*

1.
Using our collective desire –
to be near him, a handsome man –
the charismatic priest intoned,
"Everything lies in silence."

We girls, our faces up-tilted
to his inaccessibility,
pumiced cheeks,
exhaled as one.

I broke my trance –
At home, my father snapped,
*"Halt's maul! Sing mit!"*
Shut your muzzle and sing along.

What was the difference,
except the priest's promise –
our quiet compliance, our purity,
would bring us closer to God.

2.
Even then, I knew the priest
was talking through his biretta,
lying behind his Roman collar.

Grown women, we know our wombs
belong to us, who else? Not men.
Not righteous women.

Transfixed by power, high court justices
are deaf to mothers who can't survive another

child, can't feed the children they have.
Can't afford to travel far enough
to keep themselves alive.

3.
Listening, we know another silence,
which doesn't conceal but exposes
the distance between each word.
*Don't speak if you just don't care.*

# After His Murder

*in memory of a black man killed
by a white policeman.*

The night is full of marching,
looting and light pollution.
My nephew, a brown-skinned cop,
endures curses, shouts and spit
from hate-filled faces.

When I finally sleep,
dread and sadness
fill my dreaming brain.
I wake in icy sweat to hear
the rasping thrup-thrup
of an army helicopter –
so low I worry it will drop
through the roof on me.

It whirrs next door,
and searchlights bleach
my neighbor's lawn.
Shadows spread like blood.

A peace officer on Lake Street,
my nephew is hungry and exhausted,
wondering if he'll make it home alive.

## Final Loss Beneath the Sun

My dream was carnal,
making human children.
Their silky skin, limpid eyes
revealing lives they lived before –
spotted, striped, losing fins,
sprouting wings.

Babies sob when they recall
diving as Sea Lions near Japan.
Digging as Malagasy Aardvarks.
Great Auks, they swam to Iceland.
Sleeping, they hung from branches
by their tails, enjoying happy lives
as simple Babakotian lemur-sloths.

I woke praising fur, tusks, and skin,
weeping over my husband's death,
unable to think of him gone, our
grown children vanished.

When Earth's children go,
they'll leave no bones.
In the final fission,
nothing will remain.
Only the light-blasted
photos, intricate bodies
printed on gypsum, walls
people made for homes.
Outlines of creatures
who kissed, purred,
growled or quarreled.
Weeping as they hid
in caves and basements.
So many flew into the sun.

# When World Sorrow Brought Me Low

Albert Camus in his football jersey
led me to the empty stands
of his college in Algiers.
We saw the circles of hell
on a field of bones.
Ribbons of plague-blackened flesh
clung fast to tibias and femurs.

Camus gripped my shoulder.
I felt my marrow turn to chalk
as priests anointed firing squads,
telling the condemned to repent,
die, then live again in heaven.

I released my terror and plea
to the light that passed
through my closed eyes.

'Don't believe hypocrisy –
Believe in the losing game,' he cried,
'Play it with courage to the end!'

I shook my head
but who was *I?*
A person with a flit of mayflies
for a mind?

I summoned my soul,
walked onto the field,
where I met the stranger I was
and learned to love not kill her.

# How You Go On

1.
To look as if she were dead,
the last child covered her face
with her classmate's blood.
Not seeing life in her fixed stare,
the killer didn't fire.

Grieving, you peer through dark glasses.
Behind the light-blocked windows in cars,
strangers seem to lift their automatics.

Not willing to live suspecting
everyone you see or imagine,
you walk on despite your terror,
the mask you have to wear.

2.
Any ambiguous crowd,
back-lit by sun, becomes a forest.
A tree sways away, detaches
branches, trunk, sparse roots.

He's the lanky teenage boy,
a rifle or stick in his hand,
running toward you.

The distance between you
closes – he's in your face.
The expression in his eyes
shifts like a world of algae
escaping on a drop of pond.

If you call the police,
only you will survive.
If this boy has no place,
and you take him in, you'd be
captive in your home. Even so,
you trust, beyond all common sense,
that when you show your empty hands
he'll see more than fear in your eyes.

Transformation: Luminous Body
& Earth-Loving Soul

# There Will Be no Holy Place Where You Are Absent
*after Sappho*

Don't shiver waiting for angels
to stir the river or warm the ocean.

Begin your swim in cold,
displacing your weight in water.

Unspool your muscles' fibers,
your lighter body taking on
the salt of tears you hoarded
for a channel crossing.

Shed them and be done
with sorrow.

# Forever Returning

*After Louis Daguerre,
in memory of my husband*

You are running toward me, turning
with the curves of Boulevard du Temple.
Invisible, you're too quick for mercury
spirits, which Daguerre applies
to raise the living and the dead
on his silvered copper plate.

On Rue Sansone, in his open attic window,
his camera obscura traps each photon.
A quarter hour flows through 1838
as he seizes centuries of light.

Sliding sideways, you elude him.
The school boys you once herded,
through the crowded market, wait
behind the half-wall of the *pissoir*.
Vapor rises, fixed in the frigid air.

A saint said silence was the essence
of music, but *Delilah* plays on
the radio, while accordions
pause on the *porte-cochère*
of the white pensione.
You tip the quiet musicians
one franc, forgoing a croissant,
its fragrant yeasty layers, in 1968.

While angels and Parisians
move too quickly to be seen,
it's time for you to rest.
You extend each grimy sneaker

to the only other person left –
the shoe shine man, maybe me.

The River Seine hides behind the hour
that you run from Îsle de la Cité in 2043
to this almost empty *carrefour* at noon.
To a sudden radiance, as if the sun
explodes without sound or injury.

## Making Bone Lace

Future rounds the curve of her
downy scalp, her pulsing,
vulnerable fontanels.

Restless beneath the emerging
ridges of her cheeks, it raises breasts,
lengthens legs, and even skins her knees.
Lesions heal, a whirl of cells.

Light glancing off her sheen of skin,
she grows a memory of fissure in her bones,
preview of the mineral honeycomb she'll be.

The skeleton traceries of leaves,
the way light splinters and reassembles –
"Objects aren't solid. This stone,"
she tells her children, "is holey,
full of space around worlds
too small for us to see."

Knowing each atom,
a whirl of particles,
is holy and each decays,
she's not surprised when her future comes
already crazed, a Raku bowl
holding one candle.

# Late Summer Woman

*In the Berner Alps, Switzerland*

1.
She weaves baskets of timothy grass,
her eyes upon the mountains.

After building castles, her children
ruin clay towers with pails of water,
scooped from the Lütschine River,
which drains this flood-plain canyon.

On the windward-side of the massif,
her children float the stream in gentle showers.

She blames the languid valley,
where they sprawl on moss, hot sand
by mineral pools, soggy grass,
and even Alpen gravel.

She'll climb higher than the tree line
to find a place to raise them.

2.
Wearing the baby on her breast
in a woven sack, she scatters crumbs
that blackbirds swoop to gather.

Before the Jungfrau, one low fence.
Her arms are tight around the infant,
who flaps his arms to soar away from her.

To ground him, she murmurs, "balloon,"
one he'll hold in his hands and never
leave the earth himself.

She sings to him of ballast
but shapes his glides
in the lighter-than-air
silk of his future.

Sand, a mother's burden –
she is the hour glass.

# Time Exposure

1.
The losses of childhood go on
developing
in the heart's locked core.

We are children still
and we don't know
the first one we love
stays close as a breath on the cheek.

2.
When we were ten,
he was the first person
who looked inside me
through my hazel eyes, his blue.
We told each other secrets
no one else could know.

3.
I see the day Sister Innocence
warned our class about the sin of sex.

At noon, I pretended anger
with my friend and walked ahead.
He called me, but I didn't turn.

Lunch over, we came out our separate doors.
When he didn't answer my shy greeting,
I left, letting go of our friendship
for nothing but my fear.

Our school photo, out of focus
like regret – I opened my eyes too late.
The photographer caught his frown, my wince.

In a drawer marked partial recall, negatives
reverse the life we didn't have together.

4.

The darkroom light comes
from my fingers' pressure
on closed eyes.
It's not just pain
I follow when I ask
one of my possible futures
to repair the past.

5.

My tripod and camera
on shore, I open the shutter:
The wide lens shows us
floating all night on a raft
across a great but empty lake.

The time exposure slows
the changing moon.
Month by month
and year by year, it shines,
faithful to the current.

Diffused, the light increases,
opening out to hold us,
our shining edges –
an image of our lives together.

# Wonder

Recalling the bowl of antique marbles,
I see the rose and blue-bell agates,
alabasters, clays in foil, ambers
in their brown-salt glaze.

Staring back at me,
sealed in a transparent ball –
a fox, its left paw raised.

Nestled in the cabinet,
among the curios of Aunt Maxine
was a giant allie, bigger than an inch,
aquamarine on pink. "Don't touch.
This opalescent ball might break."

I loved to break the circle
chalked on sidewalk,
my thumb flicking
the cat's eye hard.
Danny Dean's shooter
jumped to my greedy fingers,
playing for keepsies not for fair.

I exchanged his cat for my tiger,
returned to my mother's Mason jar.
It wasn't yet mid-morning
in my childhood.

Far from the aggies
we shot from the taw line,
a silvery orb rolls toward me.

True Carrara with rivers of gold.
I coddle it between my palms
to warm before I hand it over.

Cupping the solid sphere,
the small boy raises his chin.
His eyes show he holds a world.

# All Senses Come Alive
*a poem sequence*

### 1. The Fragrance of Expectation
Five-years old, I tiptoed
down narrow stairs and sniffed
our shadowy living room.
Like Grandma's camphor,
the blue spruce seemed to move
closer to my nose, a scent so full of toys –
a doll, a book, a bear – that I squealed
and slapped my hand on my mouth.
If a grown-up turned the lights on,
the pine-shape might disappear.
Mom only lit the candles
to turn the angel chimes.


### 2. Hearing Multicolored Birds
Climbing a foothill in Switzerland,
we heard a rising flight of flute-like tones.
Not the common, fawn-colored nightingale,
but the rarer, olive Swainson's thrush,
his speckled chest puffed out.


### 3. Our Time Among the Bells
We dozed on the bed,
hands touching. Our baby
napped in his crib beneath
a screenless window. Zurich bells
rang low to high – Fraumünster,
Grossmünster and St. Peter's carillon.

Above the city, we were weightless
as cottonwood fluff on the summer solstice.

### 4. The Synesthesia of Emotion

Leontyne Price's ebony-velvet
tones rose, surrounded us, lifting me
with her lyric-spinto high C.

We clapped a cresting wave to her –
My palms burned and tingled.


### 5. Feeling a Place of Power

Glowing rose and sage
in Sedona, sandstone cliffs
protect saguaro growing tips.

Beneath my feet, the burnt-orange rock
transmitted a current to my hands –
thrills of grace connecting
our electric bodies
to deep earth.

# Your Spirit Comes into Being Because of Your Body
*after the gnostic Gospel of St. Thomas*

Single cell to blastula then embryo,
spirit took the shape of the child you were.

Taller than your body now,
it bends, insisting you free it

from your spleen,
your jaundiced liver,

churning stomach and intestines,
which only know waste.

As it wanders between
your heart and brain,

intuit the confusion
and open your lungs to it.

Before you free your spirit
from its house of rhythmic wind,

hold it and remember
how you felt
when you first saw it,
small and trembling in your eyes.

# Through her Permeable Body

*In memory of Ethna McKiernan*

A woman sifts the familiar world's
willows and aspen through her
shape-shifting, dappled flank.

Like the doe who drifts
in sun and shadow,
she cannot be seen
until she's unafraid.
Liminal human, she is –
in her foolish, tender skin –
still here when she departs.

She is cherished by the throngs
along the hard-packed roads.
Some limp over broken sea shells
or shuffle on arthritic feet to see her.

From beneath rusty bridges,
they praise her for the nights and days
she found them, gave them shelter.

Limestone caves below the hills
gape open, and *Bansídhe* rise to circle her
luminous body, earth-loving soul.

## Living in Flux, Being at Rest

Trudging in snow, I see how
it sweeps the low yew shrubs.
Red-twig dogwoods feather.
The willow has four flames,
despite the cold, the white.
Bright luster blinds me.

All this, but what of dying
in winter's long night.
The death we defy
is ours. We dread
the end of time.

We can only hope
in what we have.
January, our world
is closer to the sun.

Violets in my garden
will show their faces early,
warbling tones of purple,
hyacinth and yellow.

Forever is one moment
of sitting, palms open,
face turned up to the sun.

## In My Midsummer Night's Riddle

An unknown hover-craft blurs,
on the cups of a snowberry bush,
skimming the nectar-mounds of bee balm.

Camouflaged by its celerity, it whirrs –
a humming bird?

Tapering from a titanium-yellow breast
to a band of black – a bumble bee?

Rehearsing its masquerade,
this lowly actor emerges in spring –
a caterpillar, blunt-headed, hooked tail.

From its splitting cocoon – a clear-wing moth!
Puck is just a sprite.

## You Will Morph

Whether you're shedding your last egg,
or a flaky cell in your skin's seventh year,
or saving brilliant trumpet voluntaries
in music's lobe between your ears,
you're in metamorphosis.

Like a caddis fly larva, you carried
your pilfered snail shell,
reed or pebble home upon your back.

Through air, less resistant than water,
past decades of childhood, adolescence.

Through the brief day of your majority,
the hours of maturity.

Surely the minutes
of your wisdom.

Maybe the long moment
of senescence.

Next is not your death
but your transformation:

The itch you've scratched
beneath each scapula
will be wings,
healing lesion,
or grace unforeseen.

Urgent as your heartbeat.

# Invitation

Asters invite an ecstasy of bees.
As the sky darkens, their buzzing
is a wave of loose-stringed violas,
which fades in the cicada's riffing
steam, its ceaseless cymbals
like quick-sifting rice.
In the fine-grained night,
give praise for symphonies.
Love your life.

# About the Author

**Patricia Barone** lives along the Mississippi River in Minnesota and feels very lucky to have been a part of the thriving Twin Cities writing community for over four decades. With Future Rounds the Curve, Barone is publishing her sixth book. *Your Funny, Funny Face* and *The Scent of Water* were also published by Blue Light Press. Her recent collection, *The Music of this Ruin*, came from Taj Mahal Review/ Cyberwit. New Rivers Press published *Handmade Paper, a collection of poetry*, and *The Wind*, a novella.

Barone's New Rivers Press books were given Minnesota Voices Awards. She has received a Loft-McKnight Award of Distinction in poetry, a Minnesota State Arts Board Opportunity Grant for a workshop with the Irish poet, Eavan Boland, and a Lake Superior Contemporary Writers Award for a short story. Barone has published short stories in magazines and anthologies, from such presses as Wising Up Press, Peter Lang, Prentice/Merrill, and Plume-Penguin. She is working on a novel as well as another collection of poetry.